WARNING!

THE AUTHOR OF THIS BOOK HAS 22 CHILDREN
(INCLUDING 3 LOTS OF TWINS AND 3 LOTS OF TRIPLETS)
SO SHE KNOWS WHAT SHE'S TALKING ABOUT!

JUST TAKE   LOOK AT HER BATHROOM...

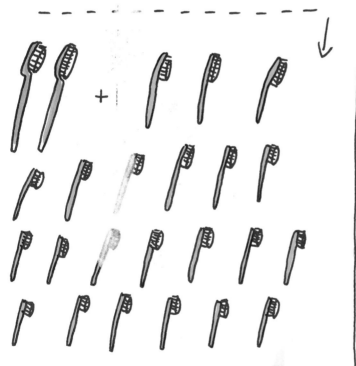

+

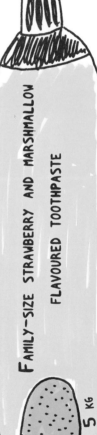

FAMILY-SIZE STRAWBERRY AND MARSHMALLOW

FLAVOURED TOOTHPASTE

5 KG

WRITTEN AND ILLUSTRATED BY FRANÇOIZE BOUCHER
(WITH HELP FROM LOU BOUCHER)

INTRODUCTION

So just how did you get your parents?

NOTE: EVEN IF YOUR PARENTS
DON'T LOOK **ANYTHING AT ALL**
LIKE THIS...

THIS BOOK IS **STILL** FOR YOU, BECAUSE
EVERY PARENT IN THE WORLD HAS STUFF IN COMMON.

TURN OVER QUICKLY TO FIND OUT WHAT THE FIRST THING IS!

NEWSFLASH!

Yep that's right, to create you your parents had sex (like billions of parents all over the world).

THEY DIDN'T BUY YOU AT THE SUPERMARKET

THEY DIDN'T FIND YOU UNDER A GOOSEBERRY BUSH

AND AS FOR THE STORK BRINGING YOU THAT'S JUST **TOTAL RUBBISH**

--> HERE'S HOW IT ALL STARTED:

NOTE: WHEN YOUR DAD'S SPERM GETS TOGETHER WITH YOUR MUM'S EGG, IT'S CALLED FERTILIZATION.

AND.............. →

THE OFFICIAL DEFINITION OF "PARENTS"

2 HUMAN BEINGS (OFTEN WEIRD) WHOSE HOME YOU LAND IN WITHOUT HAVING ASKED TO, WHO LOVE YOU MORE THAN ANYTHING ELSE IN THE WORLD AND... WHO CAN SOMETIMES BE A RIGHT PAIN IN THE BOTTOM.

THE DICTIONARY THAT TELLS THE TRUTH, THE WHOLE TRUTH AND NOTHING BUT THE TRUTH...

You might think that your mum and dad are (almost) ordinary human beings...

THEY LOOK AND DRESS JUST LIKE EVERYBODY ELSE (AND OFTEN MAKE STUPID COMMENTS).

BUT IN FACT THEY ARE AMAZING CREATURES.

THEY'RE ALSO AWESOMELY POWERFUL BIONIC BEINGS.

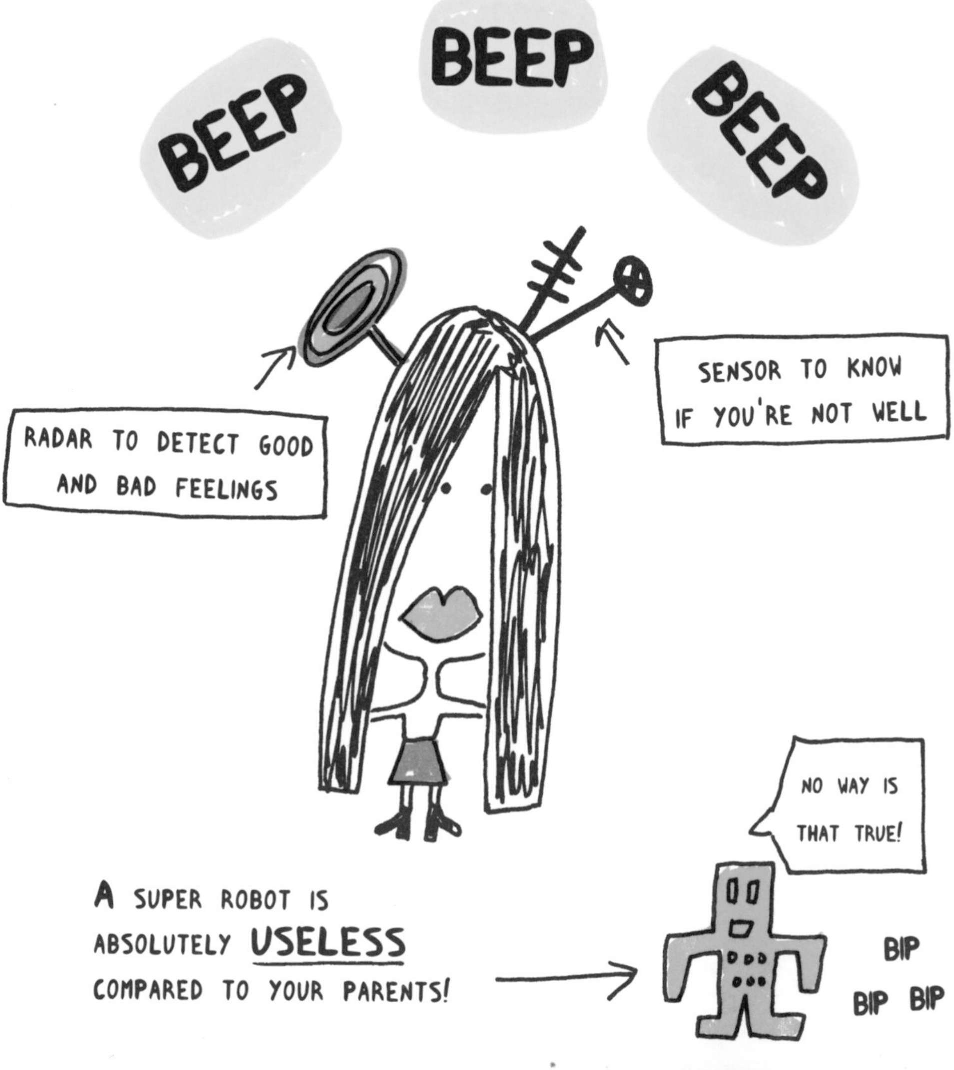

THEY'VE GOT **HUGE**, MAGIC HEARTS WHICH LOVE YOU 24/7 (EVEN WHEN YOU'RE TOTALLY UNBEARABLE).

PROOF (COMPARE THE SIZES)

PARENTS' HEART

I REALLY WANT A CHEESEBURGER.

MEGA-FAT MAMMOTH

NEVER BREAKS DOWN

HEART WHICH LOVES YOU EVEN WHEN YOU GET BAD

ALL YOUR GREENS

DON'T EAT

YOU

+ EVEN WHEN

+ SMELLY FEET

+ YOU'VE GOT

+ YOU'VE GOT BAD BREATH

+ EVEN IF YOU FEEL FAT

MARKS AT SCHOOL

UNCONDITIONAL

LOVE ZONE

ALWAYS SWITCHED ON

HEART WHICH LOVES YOU EVERY DAY

IF SOMEONE UPSETS YOU,
YOUR PARENTS CAN **CHANGE.**
THEY BECOME FIERCELY
PROTECTIVE IN ONE SECOND FLAT.

INCREDIBLE!

EXAMPLE: WATCH WHAT HAPPENS IF
SOMEONE CALLS YOU A **BIG FAT**
PEA-BRAINED IDIOT
IN FRONT OF THEM.

BEFORE THE INSULT	AFTER THE INSULT

GRRRRR

SEEING RED

YOUR MUM

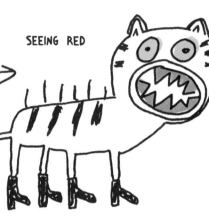

ANGRY TIGRESS

ROAAAR

YOUR DAD

VERY FIERCE LION

But **WATCH OUT** BECAUSE THIS CAN WORK BOTH WAYS. IF YOU GO TOO FAR, THEY CAN TURN INTO SCARY **FIRE-BREATHING** DRAGONS.

YOUR MUM

YOUR DAD

YOUR PARENTS ARE **SUPER SMART** AT SOLVING YOUR PROBLEMS, SO **ALWAYS** TELL THEM IF YOU HAVE ANY.

YOUR MUM AND DAD ARE YOUR ANCESTORS, THEY'VE BEEN ON THIS EARTH A LOT LONGER THAN YOU HAVE, SO THEY'VE GOT **TONS OF LIFE EXPERIENCE...**

DINO, YOUR DAD'S FRIEND
(THEY WERE AT SCHOOL TOGETHER AGES AGO)

STEGOSOMETHINGSAURUS

DID YOU KNOW, YOUR DAD FAILED HIS EXAMS 3 TIMES, HE JUST NEVER TOLD YOU?

...AND CAN GIVE YOU LOADS OF MEGA INTELLIGENT ADVICE.

MR AND MRS STONE AGE (BORN BEFORE THE INVENTION OF THE INTERNET, FACEBOOK, HIGH-SPEED TRAINS, COCO POPS® AND MOBILE PHONES)

YOUR PARENTS ARE ALSO TOTAL MAGICIANS...

1. IT STARTS WHEN YOU'RE BORN (AND THEY CAN'T GET OVER IT).

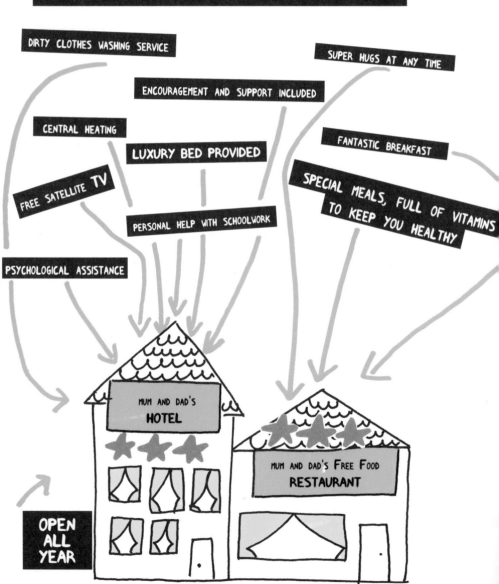

BUT <u>ALL THE SAME</u>
DON'T ASK FOR TOO MUCH...

YOU MUST BE JOKING!

FREEZE! PUT YOUR HANDS WHERE I CAN SEE THEM!

I NEED £250,000 RIGHT THIS MINUTE TO PUT A CINEMA IN MY BEDROOM.

YOUR SKI HAT WITH EYE HOLES

YOU IN <u>DISGUISE</u>

GARDEN HOSE

YOUR MUM AND DAD ARE GENEROUS BUT THEY'RE NOT MILLIONAIRES.

EVEN THOUGH IT'S SOMETIMES VERY DIFFICULT, YOUR PARENTS DO EVERYTHING THEY CAN TO **BRING YOU UP PROPERLY.**

BUT WHY IS BEING BROUGHT UP PROPERLY IMPORTANT? JUST LOOK AT THE DIAGRAM.

$\longrightarrow$

AND FINALLY, HERE'S THE PROOF THAT YOUR PARENTS LOVE YOU MORE THAN ANYTHING ELSE IN THE WORLD (EVEN WHEN YOU WIND THEM UP BIG-TIME).

HERE'S ANOTHER REALLY AWESOME THING ABOUT PARENTS.

EVERY DAY THEY DO **EVERYTHING** THEY CAN TO MAKE YOU **AS HAPPY AS POSSIBLE.**

COMPARED TO THEM, FATHER CHRISTMAS IS A TOTAL RIP-OFF AS HE ONLY COMES ONCE A YEAR.

BIG FAT COUCH POTATO.

BUT

In spite of all their super good points, your parents do still annoy you a lot.

DON'T WORRY, IT'S
NORMAL.

IT'S THE SAME IN EVERY FAMILY.

THE BAD NEWS IS...

SUPER-PERFECT PARENTS DON'T EXIST!!!

(SUPER-PERFECT CHILDREN DON'T EXIST EITHER).

SHOCK HORROR!

ALWAYS CALM
AND SMILING

ALWAYS
UNDERSTAND
YOU 100%

NEVER SHOUT
AT YOU FOR
NO REASON

BUY A CONSTANT
SUPPLY OF SWEETS

HAVE DECIDED
TO LIVE AT
DISNEYLAND
ALL YEAR ROUND

NEVER TAKE YOU
TO BORING MUSEUMS

MR AND MRS
BESTPARENTSEVER

 THE GOOD NEWS IS...

SO WHAT! IT'S MUCH MORE FUN
TO HAVE PARENTS WITH FAULTS!

HERE'S SOMETHING VERY **ANNOYING:** YOUR PARENTS ALWAYS TELL YOU TO **HURRY UP.**

⇒ OPTION 1 ⇐

GIVE THEM A DOSE OF **CALM DOWN DEAR** MEDICINE

→

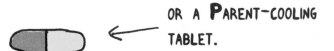

OR A **PARENT-COOLING** TABLET.

CAN YOU STOP BOTHERING ME!

HEY MAN, WHERE'S THE FIRE?

IS THERE A TRAIN TO CATCH?

OR A ROCKET, PERHAPS?

IS THE WORLD ENDING?

I ♥ BEING LAZY

RING

RING

RING

WHY ARE ALL PARENTS OBSESSED WITH GOOD MANNERS?

IT'S SIMPLE,
THEY DON'T WANT YOU TO
HAVE THE SAME HORRIBLE
EXPERIENCE AS THIS GUY.

THE FAMOUS ISTAAC MYFINGERUPMYNOSE, AGED 102.

(HE STUCK HIS FINGER UP HIS NOSE WHEN HE WAS 5 AND IT'S BEEN THERE EVER SINCE.)

HIS SPECIAL CAR

HIS HAT

AND, COMING SOON, HIS SPECIALLY MADE COFFIN

A RIDDLE

WHAT'S THE DIFFERENCE BETWEEN AN OVEN FROM THE FUTURE AND YOU?

CLEANLINESS NEWSFLASH

THAT'S WHY YOUR PARENTS ARE ALWAYS ON AT YOU TO HAVE A WASH AND **RIGHTLY SO!**

SOMETIMES YOUR PARENTS TRY TO TORTURE YOU (FOR EXAMPLE, BY TAKING YOU **TO THE DENTIST).**

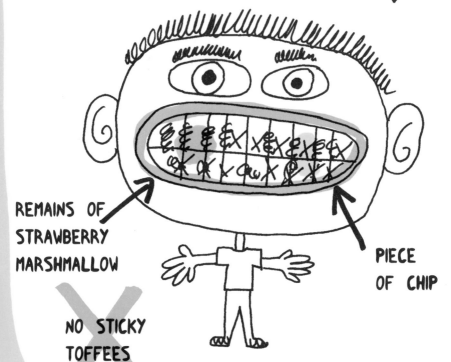

BUT IN 2032, YOU'LL THANK THEM FOR IT!

WHEN YOU'RE A
HOLLYWOOD STAR

OR THE MULTI-BILLIONAIRE
STAR OF TOOTHPASTE ADVERTS.

ADVERT

Order this fantastic machine for Christmas now

PARENTS CAN BE SUPER CLINGY...

BUT RELAX! IT'S ONLY BECAUSE THEY **LOVE** YOU.

THEY TAKE YOU
EVERYWHERE WITH THEM
WHEN YOU'D RATHER WATCH
A SILLY **TV** PROGRAMME

THEY'RE
CONSTANTLY
PATTING YOU
ON THE HEAD

SUPER
GLUE

THEY CUDDLE YOU
10 TIMES A DAY

THEY WANT TO KNOW
EVERYTHING
ABOUT YOUR LIFE

EXTRA
STRONG

THEY THINK THEY
CAN HANG OUT
IN <u>YOUR</u> BEDROOM

AND SOMETIMES THEY
EVEN SPY ON YOU!

TURN OVER FOR PROOF.

NOTE : DON'T BE MAD WITH THEM, THEY'RE JUST WORRIED ABOUT YOU (BUT IF YOU'RE **42** AND THEY'RE STILL DOING IT, THEN **YOU'VE GOT A REAL PROBLEM**).

PARENTS
ARE OBSESSED
WITH FRUIT,
VEGETABLES,
GOING FOR WALKS
AND LEARNING,
BUT **THIS IS
A GOOD THING
REALLY.**

JUST LOOK AT
WHAT WOULD HAPPEN
TO YOU IF THEY WEREN'T.

WHAT DO YOU MAKE OF THIS?

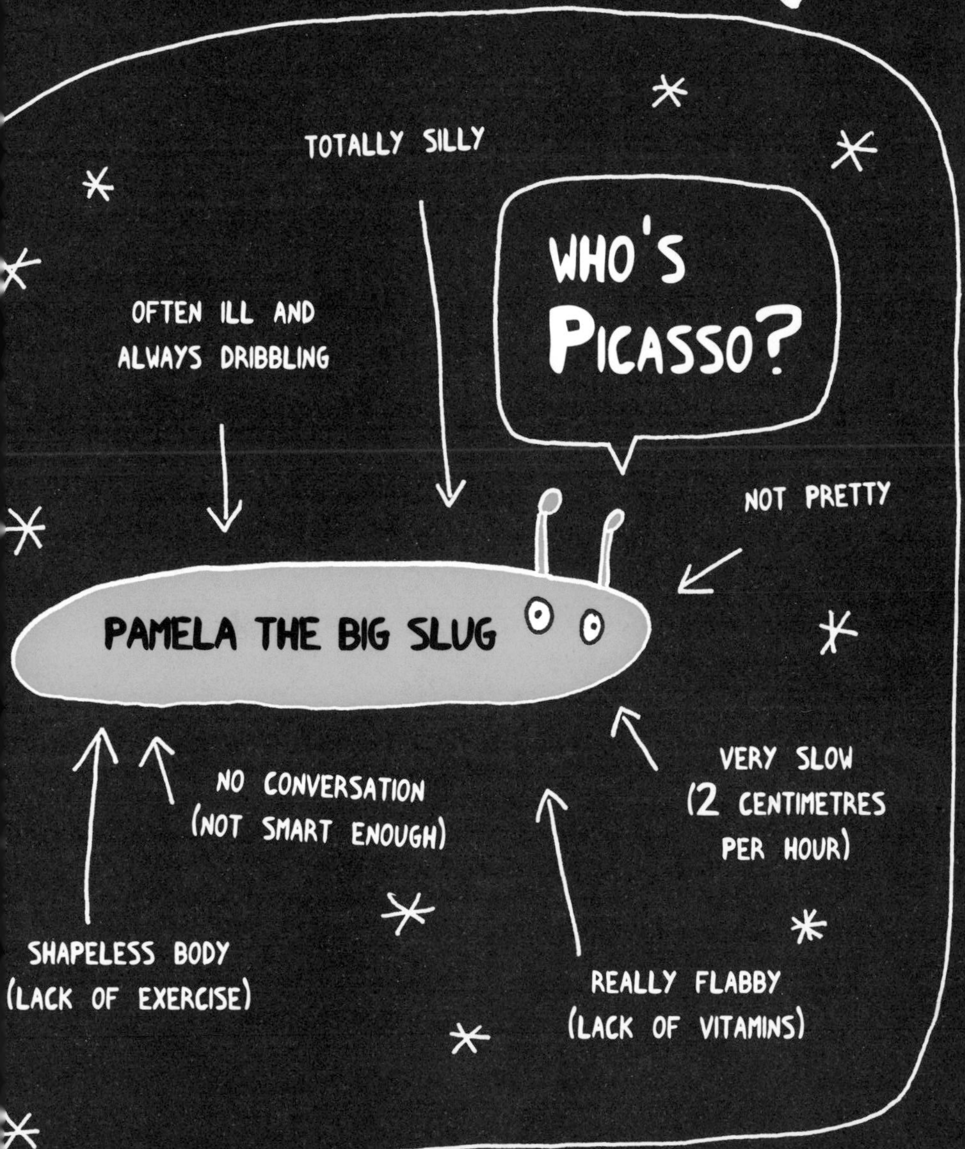

BUT AT LEAST PAMELA EATS LETTUCE!

GAME

FIND 3 MISTAKES
ON THIS PAGE.

ANSWER

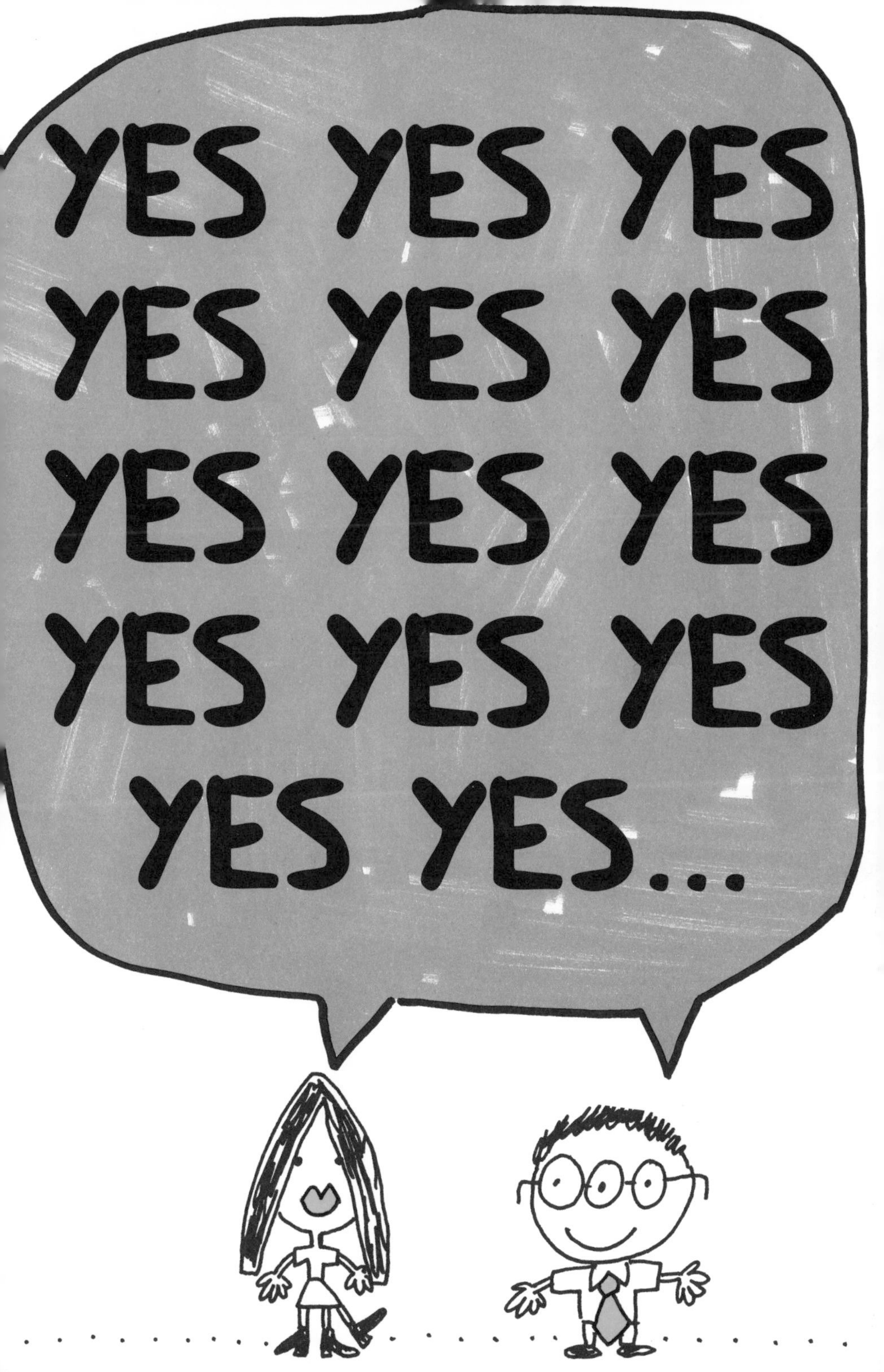
YES YES YES YES YES YES YES YES YES YES YES YES YES YES...

BUT PARENTS WHO ALWAYS SAY **NO** AREN'T NORMAL EITHER.

IF YOURS ARE LIKE THIS, GIVE THEM A COPY OF THIS BOOK RIGHT NOW.

50 FLEXIBILITY EXERCISES FOR EXTRA-STRICT PARENTS

✳ AND **WOW** JUST LOOK AT THE RESULTS! ✳

THEY OCCASIONALLY TELL YOU TO DO SOMETHING AND THEY DO THE OPPOSITE.

THE PROOF

RUN AND CLEAN YOUR TEETH, MY DARLING.

DOG BREATH

DON'T BE RUDE, ANGEL.

OH HELL! WHAT A STUPID ~~USELESS~~ WASTE-OF-TIME ~~OVEN~~ MY CAULIFLOWER CHEESE IS BURNT! *RUDE WORD*!

REMIND THEM THAT THEY SHOULD SET AN EXAMPLE!

THE TINY MAGIC WAND
THAT LETS YOU TURN YOUR
PARENTS INTO SLIMY TOADS
WHEN THEY GO TOO FAR.

ALWAYS HAVE IT
IN YOUR POCKET.

MATCH
(FOR SIZE COMPARISON)

NOTE: BEFORE YOU TURN THEM BACK AGAIN, DON'T FORGET TO MAKE THEM PROMISE TO **GRANT ALL YOUR WISHES.**

PARENTS CAN'T STAND YOU TELLING LIES, IT MAKES <u>THEM ILL</u>.

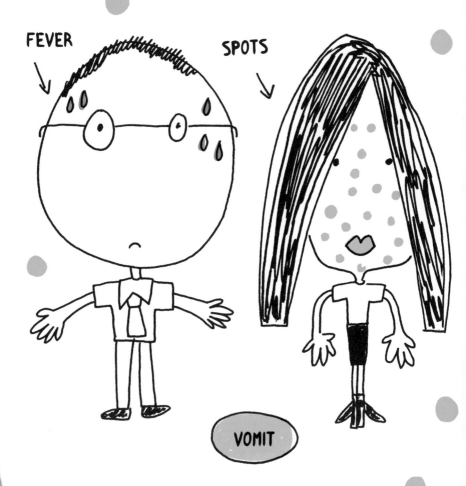

IT'S A VERY SERIOUS
ILLNESS CALLED:

SEVERE
ANTI-TRUSTITIS.

WHAT'S MORE, IF YOU TELL TOO MANY FIBS,
THEY WON'T GET BETTER AND WON'T BELIEVE ANTHING YOU SAY,
EVEN WHEN YOU'RE TELLING THE TRUTH **SO BE CAREFUL!**

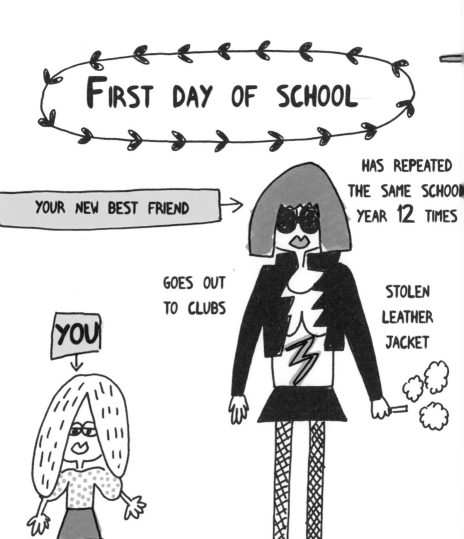

3 DAYS LATER

YOU, SENTENCED TO **6** MONTHS
IN PRISON FOR STEALING SWEETS.

IT'S OBVIOUS WHY:
THEY'RE AFRAID YOU'LL GET
IN WITH THE WRONG CROWD
AND TURN OUT BADLY!

IT'S THE END OF TERM

QUESTION: WHAT SHOULD YOU DO IF YOUR PARENTS PASS OUT WHEN THEY READ YOUR SCHOOL REPORT?

THE ANSWERS

1 MAKE THEM SNIFF SOMETHING VERY SMELLY.

2 IF THAT DOESN'T WORK, THROW A BUCKET OF COLD WATER OVER THEM.

3 FINALLY AS A LAST RESORT, CALL A SPECIAL AMBULANCE.

NEE NAW NEE NAWW!

SOS PARENTS

RESUSCITATION TEAM FOR BAD SCHOOL REPORTS

SOMETIMES THEY CAN'T EVEN AGREE AMONGST THEMSELVES!

PUT YOUR **RED** TROUSERS ON TO GO FOR LUNCH AT GRANDMA AND GRANDAD'S.

WEAR YOUR **BLUE** TROUSERS.

REALLY ANNOYING!

HERE ARE **2** DREAMS THAT **WILL NEVER HAPPEN IN REAL LIFE...**

DREAM DREAM DREAM

DREAM

WOULD YOU LIKE
ONE OF THOSE SPECIAL
TOOTHBRUSHES
YOU ONLY HAVE
TO USE
ONCE A YEAR?

DREAM

DREAM

DREA

DREAM

DREAM

DREAM
DREAM
DREAM
DREAM
DREAM
WOULD YOU LIKE 1 OR 2 MILLION POUNDS' POCKET MONEY THIS WEEK, MY ANGEL?
DREAM
DREAM
DREAM
DREAM
DREAM
WHAT A PITY!

EXAMPLE 1

HA HA HA HA HA
HA HA HA HA HA
HA HA HA HA HA
HAHAHAHAHAHA
HOHOHOHOHO
HU HU HU HAHA
HIHIHIHI HAHA!

LAUGHS STUPIDLY AND LOUDLY IN FRONT OF EVERYBODY

BAD HAIR DAY

GRANNY TOP

PLEATED SKIRT — SOOO LAST CENTURY

YOU, DYING OF SHAME

YOUR MUM

THERE ARE TIMES SOOO EMBARRASSING.

EXAMPLE 2

YOU, RED AS A BEETROOT BECAUSE YOUR DAD HAS JUST CALLED YOU 'MY DEAR ICKLE COOCHI COO' AND **KISSED** YOU IN FRONT OF **ALL YOUR MATES.**

ADVICE

TELL YOUR FRIENDS THAT THEY AREN'T YOUR **REAL** PARENTS, BUT TWO MAD PEOPLE YOU JUST MET IN THE STREET.

SOMETIMES, WHEN YOUR PARENTS GO ON AND ON... AND ON...

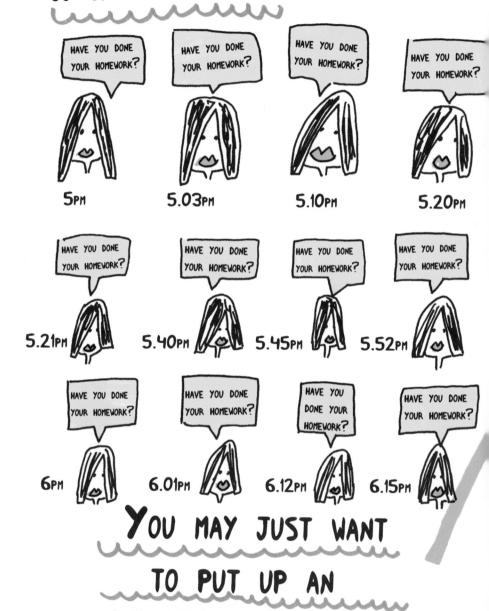

YOU MAY JUST WANT TO PUT UP AN ADVERT.

URGENT

Fantastic kid wishes to exchange parents immediately for parents **WHO WON'T MAKE HIM DO HIS HOMEWORK AND DON'T CARE ABOUT HIS SCHOOL MARKS**

BUT WATCH OUT!

IT MIGHT ALL GO HORRIBLY WRONG...

YOU MIGHT BE ACCEPTED INTO A FAMILY OF PENGUINS + MADE TO EAT RAW FISH + GET A FREEZING BOTTOM BY SITTING ON ICE ALL DAY.

OR EVEN WORSE

INTO A TRIBE AT THE HEART OF THE JUNGLE.

YOUR CHIEF-DAD

YOUR NEW DAD'S WIVES

DINNER FOR ALL THE FAMILY
(SNAKE AND
TARANTULA KEBABS)

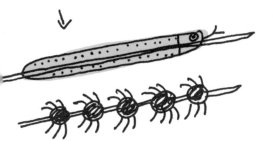

BEDROOM HUT FOR YOU AND YOUR
250 BROTHERS AND SISTERS

CONCLUSION: IT'S BETTER TO TRY
TO GET ALONG WITH YOUR PARENTS.

WHATEVER YOU DO, DON'T WORRY WHEN YOUR PARENTS SEEM A BIT STRANGE (IT HAPPENS TO ALL PARENTS).

OCCASIONALLY YOUR MUM AND DAD MAY GET FED UP WITH BEING **SERIOUS, RESPONSIBLE GROWN-UPS.**

THESE ARE SOME OF THE SYMPTOMS
OF EXTREME CASES OF
'FEDUPWITHBEINGADULTITIS',

DON'T WORRY! IT'S THE HAPPIEST ILLNESS IN THE WORLD
(AND THE AUTHOR OF THIS BOOK
HAS GOT IT BADLY).

YOU CAN EVEN GET THE STRANGE FEELING THAT YOU'RE NOT **ALWAYS** THE CENTRE OF THEIR UNIVERSE.

LA LA LA LA HIP HIP HOORAY! CIAO KIDS, WE'RE OFF TO VENICE.

LA DOLCE VITA AMORE MIO ♪♪

IN FACT, THIS IS WHAT HAPPENS...

YOUR PARENTS ARE ALSO PEOPLE
SO IT'S ONLY FAIR THAT THEY
GET A HOLIDAY TOO.

THE GREAT MYSTERY:

YOUR PARENTS ARE NEVER IN THE SAME MOOD: THEY HAVE THEIR UPS AND DOWNS.

EXAMPLE

ONE DAY THEY'RE LOVELY, BEAMING AND HAPPY.

THE NEXT DAY THEY'RE REALLY AWFUL AND IN A FOUL MOOD.

THEY LOOK **10** YEARS OLDER!

CABBAGE HEAD

TURNIP HEAD

TO HELP YOU TO UNDERSTAND, LOOK AT THE GRAPH ON THE NEXT PAGE

- - - - - >

USE THESE 2 CURVES TO DECODE AND UNDERSTAND YOUR PARENTS' MOODS.

YOUR DAD

HIS TEAM WINS A MATCH

A GOOD, RESTFUL NIGHT'S SLEEP

EVERY MONDAY MORNING

A BAD NIGHT WITH TERRIBLE NIGHTMARES

HAS A ROW WITH YOUR

YOUR MUM

LANDS A FANTASTIC CONTRACT AT WORK

BOOKS A HOLIDAY TO NEW YORK

EVERY MONDAY MORNING

THE HOUSE NEEDS HOOVERING

HAS A ROW WITH YOUR DAD

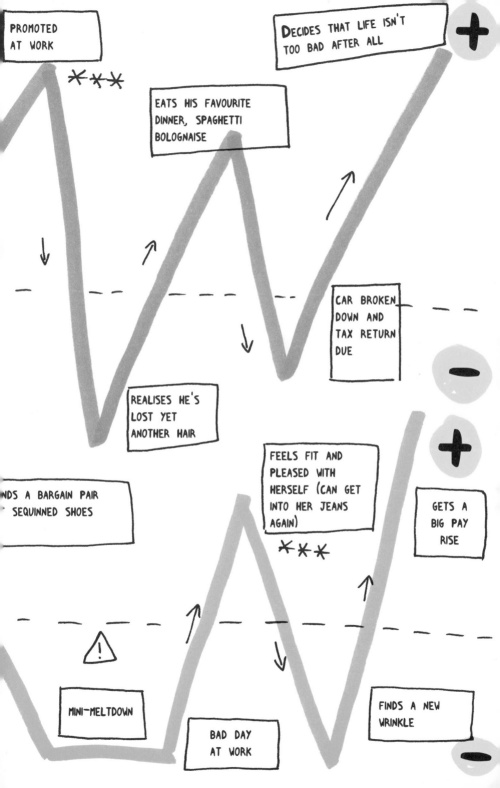

THIS IS REALLY AWFUL!

If your parents GET **REALLY ANGRY** THEY CAN MAKE **DREADFUL THREATS** BECAUSE THEY DON'T KNOW WHAT TO SAY TO MAKE YOU DO AS YOU'RE TOLD.

WHATEVER YOU DO, DON'T BELIEVE THEM!

RGI (REALLY GOOD IDEA) IF YOU ABSOLUTELY DON'T WANT TO DO AS YOU'RE TOLD.

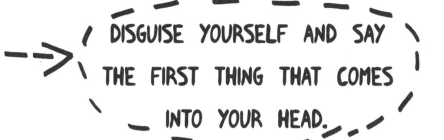

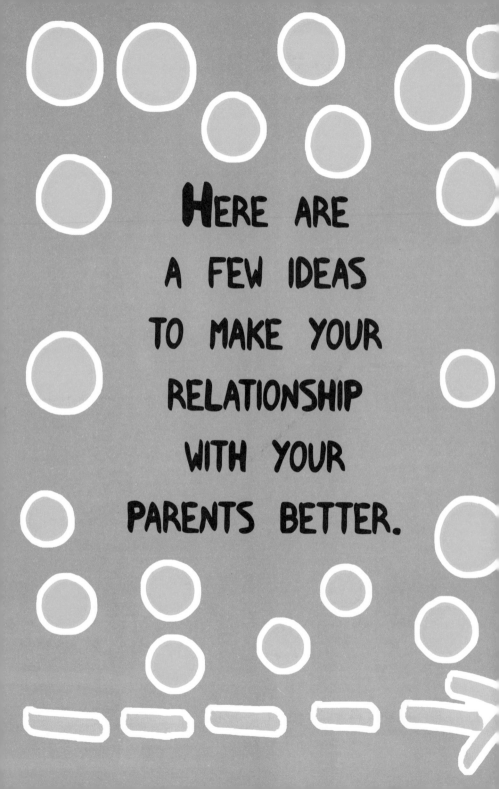

HERE ARE
A FEW IDEAS
TO MAKE YOUR
RELATIONSHIP
WITH YOUR
PARENTS BETTER.

YES (SAY THIS MORE OFTEN)

WHAT CAN I DO TO HELP, DEAR PARENTS?

NO (SAY THIS LESS)

THERE'S NO WAY I'M GOING TO LAY THE TABLE OR PUT MY EMPTY PLATE IN THE DISHWASHER. DREAM ON, FOOLS!

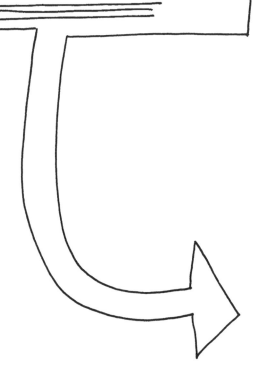

HELP YOUR PARENTS TO REALISE THAT YOU'RE GROWING UP BY SHOWING THEM THIS PICTURE OF YOU **IN 10 YEARS TIME.**

NOTE: BREAK IT TO THEM GENTLY AS THEY RISK BEING **EXTREMELY SHOCKED.**

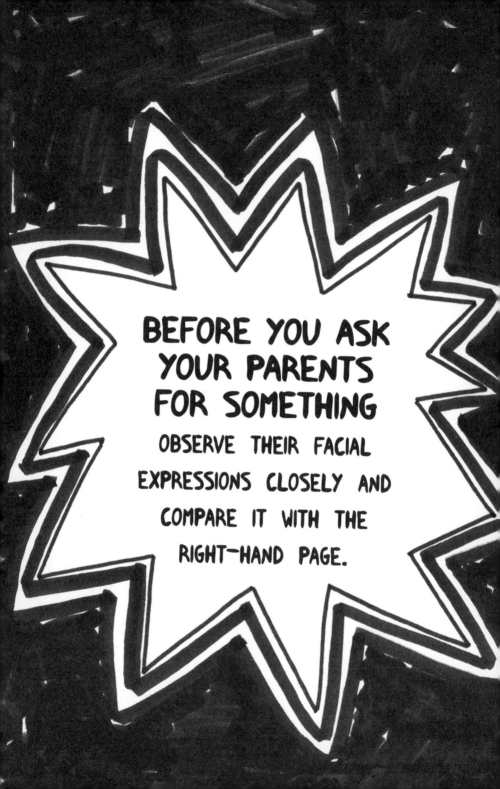

BEFORE YOU ASK
YOUR PARENTS
FOR SOMETHING
OBSERVE THEIR FACIAL
EXPRESSIONS CLOSELY AND
COMPARE IT WITH THE
RIGHT-HAND PAGE.

DON'T EVEN
BOTHER TRYING.

MORE THAN LIKELY
THEY'LL SAY NO.

GOOD CHANCE
THEY'LL SAY YES.

GO FOR IT,
SUNSHINE! IT'S
NOW OR NEVER!

WHO ARE THESE
TWO WEIRDOS?

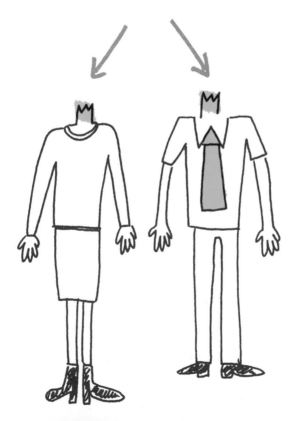

THEY'RE YOUR PARENTS WHEN YOU'VE MADE THEM SO MAD THEIR HEADS HAVE EXPLODED. SO DON'T MAKE THEM MAD AND EVERYTHING WILL RUN SMOOTHLY.

ANSWER

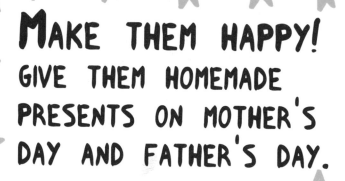

MAKE THEM HAPPY! GIVE THEM HOMEMADE PRESENTS ON MOTHER'S DAY AND FATHER'S DAY.

FATHER'S DAY

↑

UNDERPANTS MADE FROM PASTA BOWS

↑

MACARONI TIE

↑

MINI BOW TIE MADE FROM PASTA BOW

MOTHER'S DAY

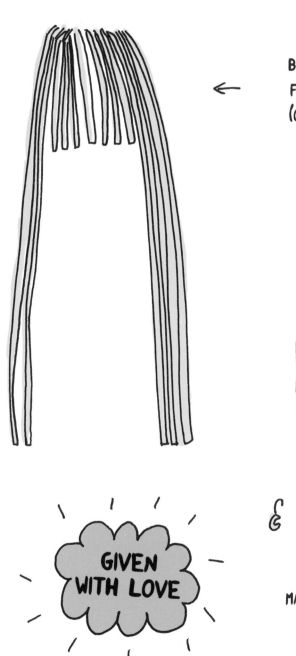

BLOND WIG MADE
FROM SPAGHETTI
(OR TAGLIATELLI)

←

GIVEN
WITH LOVE

↑

MACARONI NECKLACE
AND EARRINGS

IT'S GOOD

SOME RANDOM ADVICE

- TALK ABOUT EVERYTHING WITH YOUR PARENTS.
- ASK THEM QUESTIONS.
- SAY WHAT YOU THINK AND HOW YOU'RE FEELING.
- TELL THEM ABOUT YOUR DAY.

I HATE CAULIFLOWER.

WHAT DO YOU THINK ABOUT NUCLEAR POWER?

WHY DO YOU SAY THAT?

TO TALK!

TALKING WILL HELP YOU UNDERSTAND EACH OTHER BETTER.

AND YIPPEE!

EVERYTHING'S FINE!

TAKE TIME TO HAVE A LAUGH WITH YOUR PARENTS EVERY DAY.

EVEN IF YOUR DAD IS AN ACCOUNTANT IN A GIANT GRAVEYARD.

AND YOUR MUM SELLS
CHOCOLATE SKULLS.

HOW MANY WOULD
YOU LIKE?

HURRAY FOR HALLOWEEN!

IF THEY HAVEN'T GOT A SENSE OF HUMOUR,
TICKLE THEM UNDER THE ARMPITS
WITH THIS FEATHER.

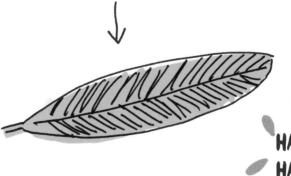

HA HA HA
HA HA HA

OR DRAW THEM.

SMILE !

DEAREST READER, YOU REALLY DIDN'T NEED TO READ THE WHOLE OF THIS BOOK (YOU'D HAVE BEEN BETTER OFF GOING TO THE SWIMMING POOL OR CINEMA) BECAUSE PARENTS ARE THERE FOR ONE REASON ONLY: **TO LOVE THEIR CHILDREN** AND ALL THE REST REALLY DOESN'T MATTER TOO MUCH!

BUT THANKS FOR READING IT ANYWAY, I'M REALLY CHUFFED!

THE AUTHOR DISGUISED AS A MUSHROOM SO NOBODY WILL RECOGNISE HER WHEN SHE GOES WALKING IN THE WOODS.

IS THIS REALLY THE END?
WELL, NO, BECAUSE THE RELATIONSHIP
BETWEEN PARENTS AND CHILDREN
IS A NEVER-ENDING SUBJECT LIKE:

THE SKY

THE SEA

LAUGHTER

IMAGINATION

POETRY

LOVE

SO, SEE YOU SOON!

Published 2014 by A & C Black, an imprint of Bloomsbury Publishing Plc
50 Bedford Square, London, WC1B 3DP

www.bloomsbury.com

Copyright 2012 by Editions Nathan, Paris, France
Original edition: Le livre qui explique enfin tout sur les parents

Translated by Gillian Williams

ISBN 978-1-4729-0472-0

Printed in China

Publisher, Nathan: Jean-Christophe Fournier
Art Director: Lieve Louwagie
Design: Albane Rouget
Proofreader: Christiane Keukens-Poirier
Production: Lucile Davesnes-Germaine and Bénédicte Gaudin
Photogravure: Axiome

10 9 8 7 6 5 4 3 2 1

PLEASE GIVE A COPY OF THIS
BOOK TO ALL YOUR FRIENDS
SO THEY FINALLY
GET TO UNDERSTAND
THEIR PARENTS!